license to carry a gun

Andrei Codrescu

Carnegie Mellon University Press
Pittsburgh 1998

These poems originally appeared in the following periodicals and the author wants to thank the editors for their permission to reprint them: "from a trilogy of birds," "a thing," "i'm careful with my dreams of death" and "leader-ship" appeared in *Works, a quarterly of writing*, Vol. 2, No. 2, Spring 1969. "testing. testing." and "winter in istanbul" appeared in *Lillabulero*, No. 7, Summer/Fall 1969. "for marg/so she could fuck again," "dream dogs," and "more love" appeared in *Pro-ject*. No. 1. Vol. 1.

Library of Congress Catalog Card Number 97-76748
ISBN 0-88748-280-5
Printed and bound in the United States of America

First Carnegie Mellon University Press Edition,
January 1998

License to Carry a Gun was first published by Big Table Publishing Company, Chicago, in 1970.

Publication of this book is supported by gifts to the Classic Contemporaries Series from James W. Hall, Richard M. Cyert, and other anonymous benefactors.

Foreword

ANDREI CODRESCU possesses the most magical imagination of any young poet I know. One sees it in action in lines such as "I want to touch something sensational/ like the mind of a shark"; or in poems of metamorphosis such as "from a trilogy of birds," "gist" and "new jersey"; or in the fact that this book is the creation of three distinct authors—a black Puerto Rican poet imprisoned for an unspecified crime, an ex-beatnik who's become a mystical Fascist in Vietnam, and a robust young woman who loves on the Lower East Side—all of whom reveal themselves in the end to be one poet, standing, elegant and ironic, in a battered garbage can. Codrescu's magic is the magic of the metamorphosis by means of which one hunts for himself by going through changes—sometimes profound, sometimes absurd or even silly—which often involve spells, runes, rituals, code words and secret messengers, complex disguises and fictitious hagiographies more revealing than mere biography. I'd even hazard the guess that this young poet's imagination has been shaped by the grand European tradition of romantics who believe that "I" can become another: the druids and alchemists, Rimbaud, Count Dracula of Transylvania, Lautréamont, the characters in the tales of the Brothers Grimm, Hans Christian Andersen and Lewis Carroll, the surrealist poets and painters, and the Steppenwolf of Hermann Hesse.

Reading these volumes and looking at the photographs

of their imaginary authors makes me wonder, in fact, if I haven't wandered once again into Pablo's Magic Theatre where all is metamorphosis, poetry at its most primary and raw.

The first volume can be seen, for example, as a magical cell inhabited by a poet who in his photo looks like one of the roughs, perhaps a revolutionary, but who soon begins to change as the cell itself changes. As Julio Hernandez tells about his fantasies of flight and peculiar symbiotic relationships with fellow prisoners and fantasy friends named Don Quixote, Melville, and the other blind man who "moves next to me/somewhere in the deeper stratas of color," we gradually learn that he is blind and essentially passive: he neither describes his sentence nor revolts against it. The cell itself turns into a womb of blackness, rain and food. Eventually the womb becomes a tomb bearing the incredibly lonely epitaph: "julio hernandez does not lie here,/he lies in your grave." Julio's metamorphosis from fetus to corpse occurs without him having left his cell.

Elegant, almost foppish, Peter Boone looks the opposite of Julio Hernandez. Instead of passivity, Peter is aggressive, often violent—a man of hunger, rage and sexual frustration. And his metamorphosis is even more bizarre than Julio's: he changes from a famished beatnik who cries out that "as usual/the tangerines are rotten/ twisted inside like a bundle/of eyes" into a mystical soldier who creates food by engaging in incandescent, ugly, sado-masochistic acts in battle in which he and his victims become the holy body and blood—as in the extraordinary poem "gist":

4

> america is healthy. i am healthy
> in the body of christ.
> the fall of melted metal builds
> my spheric soul.
> i go first.
> my body's laid flat
> on the copper table
> and pounded up thin like a sheet
> to pick up prophecy.
> six holes are drilled in my body.
> the marketing of this new instrument
> is now in the hands of pan.
> i am healthy. i wish
> that i had one thousand such instruments.

And the metamorphosis in the final volume—*Poems from the River Aurelia*—involves "the woman in the man . . . maybe the most unknown woman ever" finding out who she is. At first, Alice Henderson-Codrescu sounds preoccupied with her vitality, vanity, paranoia and derision; gradually, however, her basic tenderness emerges and one watches her change from one who needs love into one who loves and shares in poems such as "for marg/so she could fuck again," "more love," "woods, summer '68" and the superb lyric "dream dogs" with lines such as:

> years ago it was easy to dream of wolves
> and wake up your lover
> to show him the blood on your hip.

All three volumes, in turn, can be seen to comprise one book of changes. *License to Carry a Gun* is an allegory of growth, beginning with the tale of imprisonment in the womb, serving a sentence neither earned nor perhaps wanted; and continuing with the portrait of childhood sexual conflicts, including immemorial fantasies of punishment, butchering and early, melodramatic dyings; and concluding with a collage depicting difficult, energetic groping toward adulthood and love, involving also in poems such as "beach in sebastopol, california" tentative reconciliation with the ancestors.

But when I look at the cover photograph of the Pablo of these magical poems I feel chary of such critical generalization. One look at the photo of Andrei Codrescu —the 23-year-old aristocrat from Transylvania, Rumania, standing with one foot in the garbage can, grave, ironic, the very picture of the young romantic poet—reveals that he is perfectly capable of reversing the order of the three volumes or of changing the chronology within each of the books—ocean waves washing away the castle of sand which is the theory that this book is an allegory of growing pains. Moreover, his expression indicates that he is equally capable of renouncing poetry next week and becoming a gun runner or Zen monk or advertising executive or leader of a seminar on Whitehead's philosophy or Wittgenstein's sex life in a crash program for executives in Aspen, Colorado.

Such reversals wouldn't be foreign to one who has both the gift of sudden, brilliant surprise and the gift of humor which Andrei Codrescu demonstrates again and again in these poems. One example of his gift of surprise is the ending of "testing. testing." from Peter Boone's *All Wars Are Holy*: When the landlord, who appears as the classic cartoon of the enemy of young lovers in the city, suggests to the soldier, "there seems to be a question as to your existence," Peters responds: "i am happy to answer that/by punching myself in the mouth." Or take the surprise and the humor in the final image of "gang bang" where that desperate but nevertheless intimate event is likened with incomparable success to the most bland and impersonal event: "it's like a car show./there are people/everywhere."

And the wit in creating a persona and then having him dedicate a poem to one's self—as in "license to carry a gun" by Julio Hernandez—speaks for itself. As does the intimation that Andrei Codrescu is really creating the mask of the anti-poet, in that the dignified, lonely anguish of Julio, the almost psychotic turmoil of Peter, and the sensuality and tenderness of Alice's search for love are all, in the end, fictions created by a young man who chooses to pose in a garbage can.

Moreover, in the creation of his cast of characters we can also see the essence of Andrei Codrescu's romanticism. I doubt if Julio, Peter, and Alice were born as a result of the poet's admiration for the esthetics of the dramatic monologue or for the possibilities for poetry created by wearing a mask like the Yeats of "Ego Dominus Tuus" or the Eliot of "The Love Song of J. Alfred Prufrock" or the Pound of "Sextus Propertius." Rather, I suspect they were created out of an assertion that the poet is indeed a wizard or even a sorcerer who in his art can fashion whatever face or faces he chooses to wear. In brief, this is the supreme romanticism of asserting not only that "I is Another" but that I am whomever or whatever I say I am in the recesses of my imagination.

Every young poet at one time or another must wish for

such magical power to transform himself and perhaps also transform the world by revealing the secrets of the trees, animals, rocks, stars and sun, others and the countenance of the immortals. Twenty years ago, when I was first trying to learn how to write, I often felt that poetry should be able to do exactly that, and that the poet could think of himself as a witch doctor or angel fallen among Chicagoans, one whose speech becomes incantation to summon the divinities; and I remember when some poem of mine fell short of such a mark and obviously would never summon anything but a form rejection slip from *Poetry*, I would haunt the open shelves on the third floor of the Chicago Public Library, searching for that unknown magical book which would be all that I wanted poems to be. I never found that book. But when I first read *License to Carry a Gun* in manuscript, I felt that, finally, I held it in my hands.

PAUL CARROLL

The License to Carry a Gun by Julio Hernandez

All Wars Are Holy by Peter Boone

Poems from the River Aurelia
by Alice Henderson-Codrescu

THE LICENSE TO CARRY A GUN

by Julio Hernandez

for John Sinclair

The License to Carry a Gun *was supposedly written in jail by a Puerto-Rican poet. Julio is a scout into a political future of prison reality, a sacrificial lamb. He taught me survival. He was born on the Lower East Side in 1967; he is hovering saintly on the edge of all my action; hernandez like miguel and julio like my father.*   AC

Julio Hernandez
photo: Alan Dye

from a trilogy of birds

in birds is our stolen being. from summer to summer
they carry on my destruction, more obvious
as i get closer to death.
in the kitchen powerful lights stay on at night
watching the summer passage of birds.
the sea contains
their thick excrement, our longing to fly,
the sea changes color.
weak ships over the water.
i am seasonal.
i offer poisoned lights to passing birds
through the guarded door of the kitchen.
it suddenly opens.
i catch the sea when it is taken away
by disciplined clouds of birds.

fidel castro

he's got jesus dead by gun behind his motorcycle eyes,
he holds my soul on a theory bail,
rocking my country with a skinny peasant
he holds from the belt.
same peasant feeds birds at the border.
i counted so many languages in the dark
spoken by an old cuban refugee,
owner of a coca cola fountain of dead tactics,
south of havana.
my tongue is dead now,
its meat hangs like a belt
from the hand of fidel.
dubious birds
burn over the snow at the border.

i reached the limit of what they call soup
this dark garbage of jailed vegetables
and fake butter.
oh don quixote you're really my mother
diluted by soup every day
every day

a thing

it's useless to think of myself in medieval terms,
i'm not a saint, i shamelessly enjoy the meat of the prison
when it is well cooked, i'm proud
of my friendship with the librarian
who gets me *the village voice.*
i have a weak memory.
there is only one thing which keeps me
from loving this jail,
that is don quixote
when he comes to my window
and brings me postcards of ugly spanish girls

i'm careful with my dreams of death,
they should not slip into my comrades' nights,
take the place of their erotic dreams.
—a real jailer is needed for this—
paolo sleeps with his mouth wide open,
mario's left hand hangs from the bed.
i could be free if i let go for a second,
put death in their dreams.
oh dogs of silence,
i need you, senor

the license to carry a gun

to andrei codrescu

they will forever refuse you the license to carry a gun
but i am a gun and paolo and john and grazzia
(remember her forked tongue?)
the license to carry a gun is a license to be.
patricius, brutus, don quixote come naked
to my mind vs. target!
they're full of shit by daylight
but when lights go out in these cells
they are my loaded darkness,
my license to carry a gun.

**for margueritte,
real love**

people draw with their hands in the air
the way they would like to die,
that is the way they would fuck you
one after another, silver row
in fleshy afternoons of stinking jails.
but you are still my love, strange
for a spaniard to say. even stranger
for you to believe it. on your hips
that are now too large for a real baby
lie the exhaustive shadows of my hands
with power to destroy that real baby
if by god, you'd still be able

"Ilse Koch hangs herself in jail"

from *The New York Times*, 1968

jails match their people for the invisible world,
not asking them. JULIO HERNANDEZ MARRIED FOR
    ETERNITY
TO ILSE KOCH, given a house in fright
at the edge of no possible constellation.
three of their children
will return to the visible world
happy to repeat the written cycles.
. . . this poem is to beg help from he who knows
how to mutilate the black sperm of an eternal man
after the jail held its second trial.

rain

rain cuts an exit in the wall
for him who is of rain. a square hole
westward. through which the men of rain
will fly.
they prayed to water for a very long time,
they sold what they could.
the bald burglar from indiana
whose name should be silent.
silvio and his american friend, the dope pusher
from harlem, jack, one-eyed and singer
and all men who have children.
rain cuts an exit   wet like cunt
in lonely nights from very left

green

green comes from sound like milk from breast
and has a body, moral in the dark.
i lie in its arms
waiting for the creation
of internal tourist attractions.

blue

blue is female green, receiver.
blue is insects, flesh creation
in my purest darkness.
the spoons are blue in my sleep,
bordering blue on extinction.
a square of sky cut by the size
of my guilty head.

"though in many of its aspects
this visible world seems formed in love
the invisible spheres
were formed in fright"

                    herman melville

melville knew me as rapists know all about virgins
but he wasn't me, blind.
there is an invisible sphere made of love
that is color. its roots are in the east,
they're of black blood
where africa kills the negro waiter in white shoes,
where fish grow blue in sugar trees.
melville's place on earth is a furious mouth
where brotherhood is tested by removing light,
removing eyes.
it is a gift to me from human sugar trees.

leader-ship

another blind man moves next to me
somewhere in the deeper stratas of color.
he's blind of four eyes
for he moves like a leader who lost.
he is my father into blindness
here in the sweet coffee as among compañeros
in many sierra maestras.
i kiss his green hand.
it tastes like my eyes, i see through my kiss
a line of prophets, all blind.
some blinder than the others in the dark green
of his hand, crossing his lifeline
to life.

partiti sunt vestimenta mea
miserunt sortem contra me ad incarte
cla a filii a eniol
liebee braya braguesca et belzebuth*

games of cards are such that they create women
through subtle winds of chance and sweat
on foreheads; chance this time
is given to creation, of a female sort.
oh how their eyes are big, imprisoned players
when from his cards the winner gets a woman,
fucks her, right in front of the others.
she bears no fruit but nothing is wrong,
they think. at dawn
the guards take all the cards away.

* Incantation for luck in cards used by witches of the 14th
century

there is an orange rotting on the table
closer to freedom than i ever was.
i'll throw it away soon, its smell
gives me the same sweet hallucinations
i had when i was holding a gun.
orange of sun, my useless state of mind

epitaph

julio hernandez does not lie here,
he lies in your grave

ALL WARS ARE HOLY

by Peter Boone

All Wars Are Holy *was conceived as a book by an ex-beatnik who became a sort of mystical Fascist in Vietnam or somewhere else. Peter Boone is dead. He was accidentally killed when a bullet struck Garcia Lorca. They were linked by an umbilical cord 30 years long.* AC

Peter Boone
photo: John Beckerman

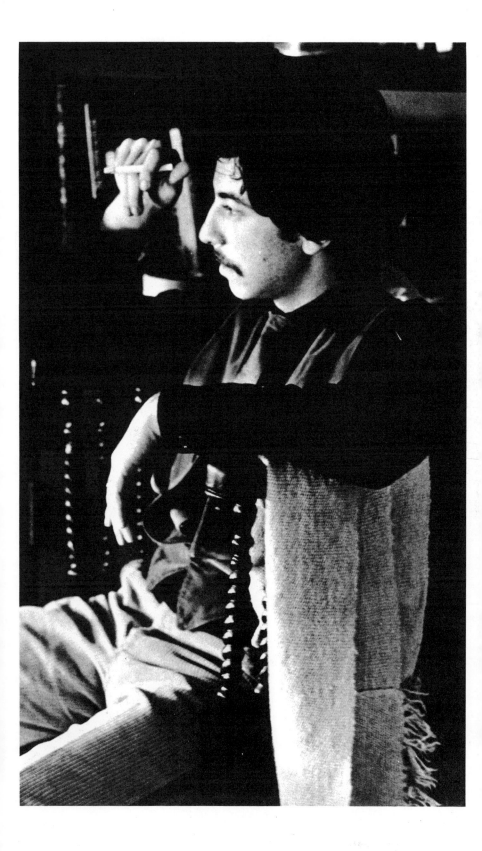

food

istanbul is a terminal city.
miles away from the stomach of greece.
the goats and the milk
are one sea away.
but my love is integral,
round like an orange on the bed table
of my youth
inches away.
there is something so sexy
about cleaning the filthiest streets in the world.
now holiness at hand
i can proclaim the end of an era,
i can proclaim my fevered body
the king of all beginnings.
soul-dirt falls here
opening a path in the beard of the saint.

winter in istanbul

such is the loneliness here.
the birds over some town in new jersey
try to imitate airplanes
and fall dead in the snow.
can't think of anything that bad.
outside the window
a moving theatre.
images of my previous winters.
a play called
freedom.
it isn't death or loneliness.
it's my capacity to wonder
fading in the dawn of the bosphorus
along with my taste for strange politics.
i should invent a woman
to shoot me with her fresh body
of winter.
farewell, black emigrant fantasy,
you who wear sunglasses at night
defending your emigrant body.
our winters meet here.
you make the birds bearable.

for sarah

i can't empty myself of you,
goddam beatnik.
i don't think you ever got to rome.
someone raped you and carved your fine bones
with fertility masks.
it's what i should've done.
your ankles make mighty fine whistles
for the lonely.
oh black messengers of birthday orgies.

womb and city

i start my fridays like a fecundity
ritual.
i throw eggs at tourists
and lift their skirts and sunglasses.
fridays remind one of birth,
of the new baby crushing against
the white walls of the hospital.
his long belly full of magic.
the body of a red cat glued to the mind
of a dead witch-mother.
fridays are the womanly ways
of this bombed city.
the mosques are golden females
and i am dying for cunt.

windows

close all four windows.
open the four windows of the body,
let your body pour in.
i hear my blood remaking you,
cleaning you of your french lessons and solitudes,
sharpening your nipples
for the battle of oz.
you're closer to me than my food.
one ra-ma   one ra-ma
passing from cousin to cousin
the sacred flame of incest.
every window is closed
in the holy town of istanbul,
every body is open in mid-universe.
i let you flow out.
it is midnight in my cunt.
you distribute the flame.

shop

they sell meat flowers in that
crazy shop across the street.
it's a feast called
the menacing babies of future events.
music from somewhere.
there is a meat flower in the piano.
this sale must run intricate ways
like illegal ammunition.
hungry turks.
in their caffeine mystery
the silent secret of . . .
that one, over there,
one hand on his hip,
the other one deep in his pocket
holding a gun.
the meat flower is now in my words
meaning music

daily

as usual
the tangerines are rotten
twisted inside like a bundle
of eyes.
fred is out in the woods
chasing nymphs,
paul is under water
hunting greek boys.
i alone
with a bundle of indian eyes.

blues are american haikus

the dead horse
holds a blue note in his yellow teeth.
the white people of turkey
pass by without looking.
minus that stare,
his death is almost complete.
it snows on a page of the
daily american
near the dead horse's mouth.
i might as well be snowed-in in a church
thinking of dead horses.
black skin brings spring.
oh how cold it is in america
since the death of its niggers.
howard johnson's is covered with snow,
dead horse hamburgers.
welcome to turkey,
black souls

gang bang

two cocks crush dry
under the flag of her hips.
there will be nothing left.
her mouth with a cherry in it
visits me slowly
every decade.
my cock is dizzy,
already aware.
the collapse
of small illusions.
it's like a car show.
there are people
everywhere.

amigaud*

antonin artaud
shaped like a broken kiss
or an abominable snow faggot
teaches english at a catholic school.
the future me is listening.
amigaud amigaud
my name is antonin artaud

* a version of "amigo"

passport

just to make sure.
wipe your ass with it
and get it right.
mayakovski couldn't say it.
too early.
a brand new russian passport.
the question of poetry never arises.

all wars are holy

what happened to me.
it isn't only this war in vietnam.
it's the war of my blood,
the small wars in immaculate labs,
the war of children in the flesh of assaba,
the wars in cosmos over the heads of philosophers.
death, magnetic void of my balance,
beloved one of my sanity,
your silk shoes are soft in the dreams of my brothers.
you finish the milk in the glass
of the rebellious husband
and give sleep to his pain-ridden mate.
don't touch me,
i am your holy mouth

gist

america is healthy. i am healthy
in the body of christ.
the fall of melted metal builds
my spheric soul.
i go first.
my body's laid flat
on the copper table
and pounded up thin like a sheet
to pick up prophecy.
six holes are drilled in my body.
the marketing of this new instrument
is now in the hands of pan.
i am healthy. i wish
that i had one thousand such instruments.

drums and believers

be true in women like a throat
made ethical by the knife.
i bleed in my drums to make her return.
the believers are tied to the drums in the night
or maybe their skin
is laid on the drums
to make her return.
i can wait like a saint
for the rhythm of my drums
to meet the rhythm of your heart
somewhere on the roads of america.
the holy beat of your body
slides white in the mind of the drums.

letter to junk jeannee

jeannee, come on.
war is good like junk.
your friends know neither.
the way you open up like a mad umbrella.
i send you an army bowl
to boil your needles in
and an ounce of grass for your friends.
i wish you could send me
one of your boobs
to keep me turned-on

note

i dream of a blitz-war of sweating teenagers,
fire-fed by black archbishops
unwinding metallic under jets.
instead, this swamp of slow mysticism,
opening windows without breaking them.
the mind yellow.
the wind of malaria
walks in like the heart of asia.
i'm in the arm of some crazy giant
who sleeps.
lazy women piss in the dust behind hutches.
but it isn't quite that awful.
nothing here is quite that awful.
the bombs
call the time for confession
under the sudden moon

the flag

the flag is an adorable symbol
who never grew up.
like me.
a horny symbol too.
erected stripes touch the forked ends
of my soul.
gulliver, beautiful imperial man,
remains the basic country.
i praise this american possibility.

letter to ezra pound

the inferno in a bacteria could be covered up
by a handkerchief. this blue scarf
will do.
yet i can't catch myself
in these trembling planes
seated as I am
on the soft bone of little infernos.
the family is at the root.
(not my family,
    since robert is almost
    ten years old,
    a small communist)
the family.
one, like in my vision of holy wars.
one, like in cunt

after meng

look black. this is the third shape of my,
this here, heart.
the half-burnt city of meng.
twisted sodom suddenly released.
where i stand
there stood a powerful woman
sure of her bowl filled with flour
biting the lips of my arrival.
the power i am after
has the intelligence of a piranha
and the solidity of heaven.

second letter to junk jeannee of nyc

now having seen so many smiles sink
into a perfect pattern of unpaid rent
and recently married meat
i want a sparkle of real-
ity. a box of it
if possible. given to me
through the telephone of your genitals
if the brain doesn't hold.
a painful sign of reality
in the name of my guts, my pretensions,
my previous lives,
in the name of 10th street and 9th street,
in the name of cheap cafeterias
and funny immortality.
istanbul? no.
under so many hats,
under elusive ribbons
the scared shit in the heart
must answer.
the scared shit must pop over and flow free.
i sit near that crack in your head
ready to release another blow

testing. testing.

whatever you say, paola francesca di virgine,
leader of mute nuns through the candles of my ideas,
whatever you desire.
see, we could turn the water pipes
into lances shields armors and crosses
and any useless offensive paraphernalia
you prefer.
half of my knighthood offers itself to you
in that sentence.
have some meat from my left arm
and all the fish from this paper bag
and my new refrigerator,
conserver of god
and of milk.
i'll stare at your cross if you say so
till i decompose.
the landlord knocks at the door
and steps on my masked face full of moss
turned blue-eyed to the mad cross
of your impertinence.
well, he says.
there seems to be a question as to your existence.
i am happy to answer that
by punching myself in the mouth.

index

i'm pregnant with potatoes and at war
with every single one of you.
somehow i hold the key.
me alone. me and me.

POEMS FROM THE RIVER AURELIA

by Alice Henderson-Codrescu

*Dedicated to all the women I have ever
known and in particular to:*

my mother
rosa luxemburg
tristan tzara
rose c'est la vie
valerie solanas
sonya tolstoy
danièle hibou
alice henderson-codrescu
myrna loy
and
aurelia munteanu

The woman in man is maybe the most unknown woman ever; this fascinated and obsessed me for a few years. At one point in California, the woman came back to me; this book is the beginning of my search for this Lady in English. The feeling was of a "notice of health" from the River Aurelia, a river which has never been sick, polluted with melancholy.

The River Aurelia is fictitious, but it flows nevertheless: its name comes from Aurelia M., my first wife. Four years ago in Rome, I wrote a long epic poem in which I established a new mythology: of moon worship, anti-civilization, permanent migration, permanent revolution: the women go under the earth to build a female world while outside, in the sun, men make themselves women of salt. That myth reverberates several times in the book. That much for genesis.   **AC**

Alice Henderson-Codrescu
photo: Andrei Codrescu

reverse

a poem for rosa luxemburg who lost it all one summer
but next there it was,
on the other side of a gilded german window.

i, too. born on the other side, alongside
an intricate, painful brain,
in the deep snows of the barbarian kingdom,
a state of permanent sorrow.
the horses unmoved in the warm stables.
beat the ground you were born on,
lash it with your later female skins,
screw your breasts into it,
unveil, unearth.
a country of women.
at some depth we find each other, rosa,
i find your profile obsessing hamburg,
moscow and london.
i'm not nervous any longer,
nerves are short and the longest bone in my body
is black, the longest
year in your memory stops short
of witchcraft.
there is alcohol in your blouse,
revolution is alcohol left over,
the countryside is still fermenting it.
tastes like hell.
rosa luxemburg,
i'm cold and new york is a white city.
the warm glove of your assassin's hand
lies on my table,
dinner for a friend

ZZZZZZZZZZZZZ

i want to touch something sensational
like the mind of a shark. the white
electric bulbs of hunger moving
straight to the teeth.
and let there be rain that day over new york.
there is no other way
i can break away from bad news
and cheap merchandise.
(the black woman with a macy's shopping bag
just killed me
from across the street.)
it is comfortable to want
peace from the mind of a shark.

s.d.s. meeting

i, feeling naked,
(though i have on my best dress and red shoes)
throw grenades from your moth-covered mouth
at an invented congress in your bathroom,
oh vladimir ilyich lenin.
oh how your back itches
but you have to keep opening your briefcase
to pull out the papers of the future.
i have dreams of bums pissing over your briefcase.
you have an ugly body,
you're probably german.
your muscles are jammed with decisions.
the beards of your followers
smell of the bowery
and i am truly yours NAKED

imported days

some days, like birthdays, are imported
from france, honolulu and bangkok.
you stretch them out by minutes
and enjoy every piece
while buildings bury themselves in the ground.
you grow in and out of a mailman,
a cosmic mailman
from the african or indian market of birthdays.
the sky of this has a hole in the middle,
it pours feasts!
never again beyond into the banal

new jersey

in the red woods my belly is red. i shall
assume supreme command of my execution,
i remember these woods from childhood.
you do it slow
so the beast in the knife doesn't get frightened.
my blood will visit you later
to tell you the story and how to forget it.
shove it under the stairs when it darkens
and its teachings are done.
my blood isn't there to coagulate.
it moves to the bellies of supreme statues.

**for marg
so she could fuck again**

i want to clean the lover of the dead warrior
take that strangeness out of her
like a poisonous herb
for my hands to remember.

if you lived through the livers of warriors
kneel near those ladies locked in their hearts,
cut the chain between their knees.
clean prayer, lord of thighs,
make your body go past
the black iron balls of the hero,
past the half-eaten subway in the fork of his memory.
the rats and the rain like an envelope.

i kneel and i clean you,
i put back the flame in your cunt
out of my own.
let's move to the rhythm of my body,
over the lordly gold of the dead in the rain

1st avenue basics

if you fight guerrilla warfare in a green skirt
down 1st avenue
leave your breasts at home.
that goes for running guns too.
perfumed high-class mouths blow pearled-handled
    pistols.
these are the basics of 1st avenue.
the beauty in the hand. basics for a new poetry.
then you warm to your heart
kleenex used by maria dolores.
this helps you erase every trace of your passage.

reverse

the storm outside
must be the kind you read about in the newspapers,
killer of babies and bums.
the kind of rain that goes on in the subway
when i hold on to the coat of a fat man
whose disastrous life
makes me happy

dream dogs

years ago it was easy to dream of wolves
and wake up your lover
to show him the blood on your hip.
the wolves had ties
and followed after every sentence
rather polite.
now there are police dogs
using tear gas and the lover next to you
doesn't wake up.

dawn

three times, yearly, my breasts dawn painlessly
into a cycle unknown,
i am struck.
a thing like dawn escapes the hand,
blinds the hypnotist,
throws the witch in wild confusion.
poetry, its opposite.
my lower body crawls with beggars
like a medieval city prospering in the ruin of its
    neighbors.
tea merchants getting fat.
my mind, restructured to resemble a gun,
a miraculous gun of known deeds, heroic
resemblances. the upper hand
of affinities.
i, like a merchant, fat,
i roll by on a thick carpet, touching,
untouching.
i love to scream in mornings like this,
to awaken a dawn ancestry

spain

my south window uncovers babylon as it looked to iram,
the golden beggar of fifteen diseases.
my south heart opens in the drive-in mouth of america
seen through the eyes of her black girls.
south facing south, i remember
a room without south,
hotel pescadore, 1965

will and power

come back from the congo when i say so. i love
to crack those hard memories. the days
without control. the third-rate poets eating rats.
the thursdays of your feet stretching
to a happy summer. but ha,
the sea is deaf when my prick is harder than stone
and soft is the bone
when the prick takes care of the sea. flatter
the lord, whoever he is. involved with the law
like a waiter. court cafeterias. armpits
of soldiers. let's set the clock for the hour.
nothing reaches us now. they are late,
so late, oh, so late.

heart breaking times

talk to me when i suck out your karma with the tip of
    my tongue,
wasting your vital lemonade on my bored limbs,
killing your cat too
for a third consequence.
if i hang myself from the head of your prick?
if i stab myself in the heart with it?
you'll go on screwing until
my meat is cleaned out and the bones
rattle no more. oblivious.
such death happens a lot on this side
of the female forehead.
you're nothing. a book of matches
lies on a mahogany table. the girl of the house
lights her hair. "i want a good lay"
she seems to be saying or maybe
she's someone else. these
evenings . . .

breast vibes

in the gynecology cell in the heart of the night
my eyes scream like a baby,
a brutal you stands up, it claims my eyes.
i enter your belly.
we shake like motel beds in a tangle
of umbilical cords
and the doctors shiver outside,
their fingers are freezing

woods, summer '68

for theo

your flashlight pins me down like a tomato
ready to be squashed by a shoe.
the light is a beast, the trees are foul,
their bark unfolds and imitates the skin.
my body's resting, leave it clean,
get out. i manage well.
and all of it is mine, the river
listens, the trees unroll.
you, take your prick back to the city,
back to the stone.
the flashlight breaks. a better beast
pours in the space, around my bones.

debts

the onion tears fall from the eyes of saints.
i have to pay or crack open.
life is salty, this room is hot. how i long
to poke a saint in the nose.
bravado, king of non-existent spain
winds by, his face is young and soon he, too
will be a bunch of tears without a face to punch.
i belong to a more subtle *it*, more nervous,
knowing not how to wait, living in a small room
full of blood and of books.
i pay with colored shells, sharpened at ends,
nothing remains coupled for long.
the tears are spent and our fathers were
11 years old when we got born.
then war came as a proof that neither spain
nor kingdoms do exist.
the tears are sperm. the knife in the purse
is insane.

more love

wheat grows from your left cheek, vastly forbidden
and hot bread comes from your mouth. regardless of
    cycles
as they draw calendars. same lines on the palm
of the left. yours, blue,
mine, thick, both sensuous their way.
you've been eaten up to the waist
in the shape of the spanish republic. of me
there is only this mouth on your shoulder,
this hand and this poem

i visit brooklyn with a queen in mind

and there, sir, comes a rehearsal of history
when the ring turns purple on the finger of the queen.
she takes off in a halo of pain,
sick like a lemon and stumbling
over the kosher butcher shops of this area.
throughout the earth everywhere
she is accused of witchcraft and death.

her body is well known to many men of her time
and it hangs over them like a seal,
it marks them for delivery.
another seal, smaller, moves inside her seal,
it is secret and hot.
what queer history floods us, sisters.

take matches, for instance, they have been
the closest to your dying flesh
and yet we don't know one another.
the matches light the stove,
the food is quietly cooking.
guard the virginity of brooklyn.
no matter what it holds it is sick.

beach in sebastopol, california

whoever found this beach alone, maybe in 1723,
was beautiful: a young indian
who laid his girl in the sand, smoked some,
barked at the sea. the fishes, the firecrackers
of the sea going out at his feet.
damn all time, even his. even then
someone was dreaming already of building new york,
within horses
cars were stirring. now, i love him
whoever he was in 1723. i ride
his horse, he drives my volkswagen,
i am his,
he discovers my beach and we sit at the sea
and the breeze opens books.
the hooks of the occult jam the sewing machines.

poem for kyra

paradise too is a schizophrenic slum,
a holy octopus with rooms to let
and the four rooms on the left are taken,
it smells as if they are frying angels in there.
in here you smile,
cheat the barefoot goddess at dice,
she doesn't know any better
she's busy unbuttoning your shirt,
feeling your thigh.
you lean on her breasts,
you're maybe ready to die or maybe
it is only dice you're going to play.
for the sheep no danger.
unless you go farther
or take me with you.
then paradise: a thousand strong women
armed with flamethrowers and loaded pussy
storming the streets of the world